Lincoln

A DOG WALKER'S GUIDE

Catherine Smith

COUNTRYSIDE BOOKS
NEWBURY BERKSHIRE

First published 2015
© Catherine Smith 2015
Reprinted 2018

COUNTRYSIDE BOOKS
3 Catherine Road
Newbury, Berkshire
RG14 7NA

To view our complete range of books,
please visit us at
www.countrysidebooks.co.uk

A CIP record for this book is available from the British Library.

ISBN 978 1 84674 324 5

All materials used in the manufacture of this book carry FSC certification.

Cover picture supplied by
Roger Evans

Produced through The Letterworks Ltd., Reading
Typeset by Jean Cussons Typesetting, Diss, Norfolk
Printed by The Holywell Press, Oxford

Contents

Walk

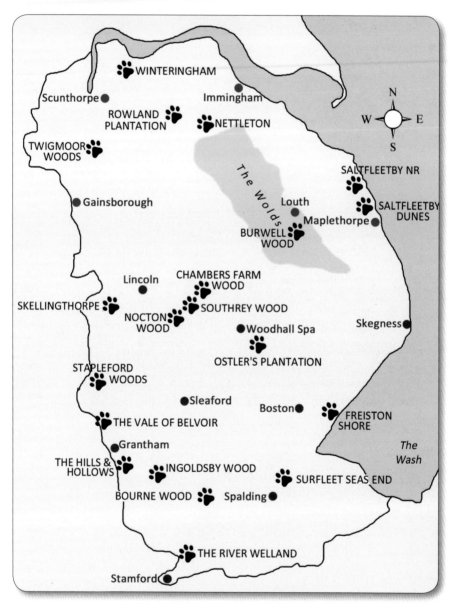

Area map showing location of the walks.

INTRODUCTION

The wonderful thing for me about having dogs is the companionship they give you on a walk. Also, of course, you know your dog is enjoying the experience in the great outdoors even more than you are!

My dogs enjoy nothing more than the excitement of exploring a new place, off the lead and able to roam at their leisure. They are always exhausted at the end of the day, free to dream of the woods they foraged through, the meadows they ran across or the rivers they swam in.

The best dogs walks offer the following:
- Circular, with simple to follow routes.
- With minimum exposure to livestock.
- Dogs free to roam off the lead.
- Away from busy roads.
- In a varied landscape with great views.

Lincolnshire is very special, and yet is often dismissed. It sits there quietly, modestly, serving its purpose to agriculture, RAF stations and the great north-south fast train links. However, as one of England's largest counties it is also one of the most diverse and extraordinary areas in England.

The county doesn't offer only one type of walk – there's a bit of everything! Lincolnshire is divided into several areas, the Vales, the Fens, the Wash, the Wolds and the North. Each area of beauty brings with it a diverse type of walk. The lush green vales to the south-west provide wonderful canal walks and beautiful hilly countryside. The Fens to the south-east offer the chance to see a wetlands habitat and the wildlife it supports. The Wash brings us wonderful coastal walks all year round. The wonder of the Wolds in the middle of Lincolnshire has stunning woodland and quaint towns. The north brings us close to the moors and peatland while around the whole of the county are farms of every type. And not forgetting Lincolnshire's famous RAF history which is evident throughout. From the Red Arrows at RAF Scampton outside Lincoln, the history of the Dambusters at Woodhall Spa or today's East Coast bombing range, Donna Nook, near Mablethorpe.

Any dog owner knows that walking is not just about spring and summer. It's about walking all year round and watching the seasons change. The coast is wonderful for walking in winter, seeing the woods change colour in autumn, the new life on the canal in spring, and watching the farming during summer and harvest.

Walking the great outdoors with your dog is fun for the whole family. Lincolnshire offers you all that freedom and adventure.

Catherine Smith

*The author with her two cocker spaniels, Hamlet
and Gracie, enjoying Woolsthorpe locks.*

PUBLISHER'S NOTE

We hope that you obtain considerable enjoyment from this book. Although at the time of publication all routes followed public rights of way or permitted paths, diversion orders can be made and permissions withdrawn.

We cannot, of course, be held responsible for such diversion orders and any inaccuracies in the text which result from these or any other changes to the routes, nor any damage which might result from walkers trespassing on private property. We are anxious though that all details covering the walks are kept up to date and would therefore welcome information from readers which would be relevant to future editions.

The simple sketch maps that accompany the walks in the book are based on notes made by the author whilst checking out the routes on the ground. For the benefit of a proper map, however, we do recommend that you purchase the relevant Ordnance Survey sheet covering your walk. The Ordnance Survey maps are widely available, especially through booksellers and local newsagents.

ADVICE FOR DOG WALKERS

As an owner, you have a responsibility for your dog and its behaviour. You know your own dog, but there are times when you need to think ahead and be prepared to take quick action.

- Always put your dog on a lead when walking through livestock. The farmer is in his rights to shoot your dog for worrying sheep. Don't take that chance, especially during the lambing season.
- Cattle can be intimidating. Keep your dog on a lead close to you and walk briskly if you have to cross a field of cattle. If they come too close, drop the lead and let your dog run ahead – he'll be much quicker than them. Never walk between cows and their calves, they're very protective and may charge.
- If you approach another dog walker whose dog is on a lead, put yours on a lead too. Their dog may be aggressive, in season, or vulnerable.
- Clean up after your dog. Always take poo bags with you and bin the bag. Also worm your dog regularly.
- Ensure your dog is micro chipped and wears a collar, just in case he wanders off in his excitement.
- Dogs love to be off the lead and free to roam. Ensure you always know where he is and keep him in sight. Remember, some children (and adults) are scared of dogs and some breeds can be over familiar with strangers. If a child wishes to stroke your dog, kneel down beside the dog and supervise the meeting if you trust your dog.
- Remember to abide by the rules of restricted access. Nature reserves either do not allow dogs in, or expect them to be on a lead. This is to protect the wildlife. Popular beaches can have restricted dog access in high season. The beaches recommended in this book are dog friendly all year round. Most UK beaches permit dog walking between September and April, however, things can change at a moment's notice, so I would always advise you to check first with tourist information before visiting.
- Never leave your dog in the car. If a dog is in a hot car and seen to be in distress, the public have a right to break a window to rescue it. Dogs can overheat very quickly in a car, even if it is parked in the shade. Always travel with water for your pet.
- If your dog falls ill, I have given contact details for the nearest vets at the end of each walk.
- Remember that routes and use of fields can change. If in doubt, always follow the yellow way-markers.
- Distances in the book are given in metres, but if you prefer the imperial measurement, 1 yard is just short of 1 metre.

Winteringham to Whitton

Walking along the estuary.

We begin at the very top of north Lincolnshire alongside the river Humber with views of the mighty Humber Bridge in the distance. This walk gives your dog the opportunity to get close to water and run through meadows. On a hot day there's a welcoming breeze along the estuary as you walk on the embankment towards the charming village of Whitton. The second part of the walk takes you across meadows and arable fields, down quiet tracks and country lanes towards Winteringham. This is a lovely walk in spring and summer when the fields are awash with golden corn.

Terrain

Flat and uneven in places. Can be muddy underfoot when crossing fields after wet weather.

Where to park

Verge-side parking on Low Burgage (road) near Winteringham Haven. **OS map:** Explorer 281 Ancholme Valley (GR: 934 227/Sat Nav: DN15 9PE)

How to get there

Take the B1207, then Winterton Road, following signs to Winteringham. On entering the village, drive through until you see The Bay Horse Inn on the corner of Low Burgage. Continue along Low Burgage and use verge-side parking towards the bottom.

Nearest refreshments

The Bay Horse Inn & Restaurant, Winteringham DN15 9NS www.bayhorse-Inn.co.uk. Dogs are not permitted inside during lunch and dinner when food is being served. However, they are allowed in the beer garden.

The Walk

. . . .

1 Start by walking down **Low Burgage**, which bends to the left and crosses a bridge towards the **Humber Yawl Club** signposted on your immediate right. Here you will see some wooden steps beside the noticeboard for the **South Humber Heritage Trail**. Climb the steps and go through the gate to follow the footpath towards **Humber Bank**. This grassy path parallels the track for the Yawl Club.

2 After walking this short track, you will meet another public footpath sign for **Whitton**. Turn left and follow this footpath which crosses a track towards

Dog factors
. . . .
Distance: 5¾ miles.
Road walking: Only on quiet lanes.
Livestock: Horses, penned off at point 5.
Stiles: 3.
Nearest vets: Winter Swan Veterinary Centre, 7 High Street, Winterton DN15 9PU ☎ 01724 735003

a gate. You continue ahead towards Whitton for the next 2½ miles along a grassy embankment beside the estuary. There is only one bench on this embankment which is at the start of this path. Towards the end you meet a large tree overlooking a pond which has clean water for the dogs to refresh themselves. It makes for a pleasant rest stop here where you can see the mighty Humber Bridge in the distance behind you.

③ **Humber View Farm** in Whitton is on your left as you reach a gate at the end of this 2½ mile ramble. Cross the stile by the gate, following the way-marker. There is a bench here for a rest stop, beside the information board. Otherwise, turn left, and then right on to the road through this small charming village. Walking past a row of houses on your left, you climb the road towards the church and turn left where you will see a public footpath sign which skirts along the outside of the church grounds. The footpath comes back out onto **Chapel Lane**. Continue ahead towards the red telephone box on **Post Office Lane**. At the telephone box, turn left beside the public footpath sign and follow this narrow, leafy lane which opens up into a meadow.

④ Walk through the meadow with the hedge line on your right for approx 100m until you reach an opening on your right. Walk past the stone post and turn left onto the track where the way-marker here is buried in the hedge. At the end of the track it curves round to the left where there is a stile and a fence.

⑤ This field holds horses in field sections, so put your dog on a lead for this short section as it has a live fence. Cross the stile and walk approx 200m diagonally across the field towards another stile at the end by the hedgerow.

⑥ Cross the stile and walk ahead through an arable field. A clear compact footpath has been made through these fields by the farmer so walk towards the way-marker on the hedge at the end. This field can be very muddy underfoot after wet weather, so wellies in winter!

⑦ At the end of the field, turn left on to the road known as Ings Lane then at the T-junction, continue ahead. At the end of this road is a public footpath sign for **Water Side**. Turn right here.

⑧ You now follow the grassy track as you pass red farm buildings, then a field drainage ditch on your right. The field curves round to the left across a wooden bridge into the next field and you continue ahead until you reach another bridge with a way-marker that takes you on to the next section of field. Turn right and follow the arrow.

9 At the end of this field is a public footpath sign **Water Side**, before turning left on to **Rotten Sykes Lane**. At the end of this lane is a T-junction and at the signpost turn right towards the public footpath 'toward church'. *(Note, you can shorten your walk by continuing ahead instead, which will lead you straight back to the start point.)* Follow the footpath for 600 metres which leads you towards the village church. There is another public footpath sign where you turn left towards the church, then cross a small wooden bridge. Follow the path towards the church.

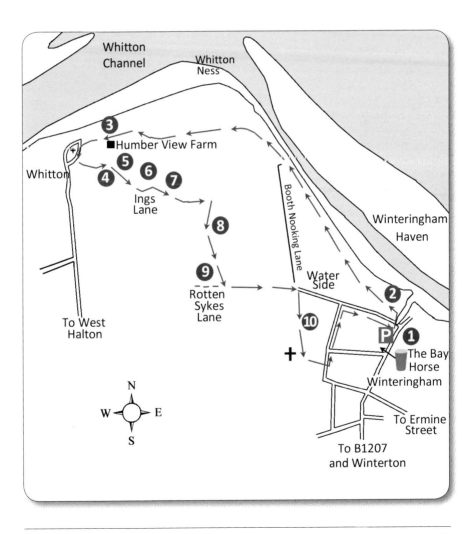

Lincolnshire – A Dog Walker's Guide

10 At the next footpath sign, turn left into the village, and then left again on to **Meggitt Lane**. At the T-junction turn left on to **Western Green** by Corner Cottage. At the next T-junction, turn left on to **Marsh Lane**. Here you will see a bridge with white painted rails. Cross this bridge and continue ahead until you reach the T-junction. Turn right on to **Water Side** and follow this road back alongside the Humber Yawl Club and back to your start point.

Splashing in the pond along the estuary.

Exploring Rowland Plantation

Ready for an adventure.

Rowland Plantation is part of a network of woods between the villages of Appleby and Broughton. This north Lincolnshire wood offers good footpaths for year round walking and the option to explore deeper into more hidden trails. For almost 100 years, the towering pine trees have made this a striking wood that will keep your dog on his toes. There are benches in the wood for pleasant rest-stops as you enjoy this 1920s masterpiece. Your dog will particularly enjoy exploring through the ferns in these vast woods, and there is an opportunity for him to swim in the pond.

Lincolnshire – A Dog Walker's Guide

Terrain
Good all weather walk. Flat, even terrain.

Where to Park
Rowland Plantation has a small car park **OS map:** Explorer 281 Ancholme Valley (GR: SE 954 121).

How to get there
Rowland Plantation lies between Broughton and Appleby. From Broughton, drive along Ermine Street towards Appleby (B1207). You pass a crematorium on your right, then a right junction for the B1208. Continue ahead for another mile until you see the next right turn which is quite small and leads you to Rowland Plantation's car park. *If you reach the railway crossing, you have gone too far.*

Nearest refreshments
The George Hogg, Market Street, Winterton DN15 9PT is a friendly pub that welcomes dogs in the bar area and serves food. ☎ 01724 732270

The Walk
· ·

1 From the car park, walk through the wooden gate with the way-marker, into the woods and continue ahead along the footpath. After half a mile, there is a crossroads with a bench for a rest stop. Continue ahead for another half a mile until you approach the end of Rowland Plantation, marked by **Lodge Farm** on your left and the B1208 ahead.

2 Put your dog on a lead as you go through the gate and cross the B1208. On the opposite side go through a gate where the public footpath is marked **East**

Dog factors
· ·
Distance: 4¼ miles.
Road walking: cross the B1208 between the woods. Quiet road.
Livestock: None.
Stiles: None.
Nearest Vets: Winter Swan Veterinary Centre, 7 High Street, Winterton DN15 9PU ☎ 01724 735003

Wood and there is a sign for **Clapgate Pits Nature Reserve**, as you now skirt the edge of **Far Wood**.

3 Go through the opening in the fence on your left, which leads you to open fields. Turn right and walk along the edge of the field with the hedge line on your right. You will see (and hear!) the dog sanctuary on your left as you skirt the edge of this field.

4 At the end of the field by the telegraph post, turn right towards the way-marker sign, across the track, and back into the woods on your left. You are now entering **East Wood**. As you walk through this wood, bear left, crossing the small wooden bridge and you will see a footpath sign **Brigg Road**. The bridge crosses a small stream with clean water for your dog.

5 After crossing the bridge, you meet a fork in the path after 50m. Bear left, following the fence line. At the next crossroads is a public footpath sign, turn right here, walking back into the woods. At the end of this path, you meet a T-junction by a footpath sign and turn right. After 100m, you meet another crossroads, turn right again. At the next T-junction, bear right and continue ahead at the next T-junction. Where the path forks, bear left. You are now approaching the fence line by the bridge you previously crossed.

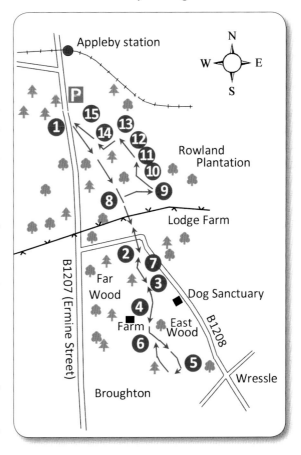

6 Cross the bridge and continue ahead. By the footpath sign is a clear pond for your dog to splash in. Now turn right, pass the pond and bear left at the footpath sign. Continue back along this path through East Wood. On leaving the wood, cross the track and walk back along the field which skirts Far Wood with the dog sanctuary on your right.

7 At the opening of the wooden fence, walk back into **Far Wood** and turn right, back through the woods towards the main gate on the B1208. Put your dog on a lead as you cross the road and re-enter Rowland Plantation.

8 Back in Rowland Plantation, continue ahead for half a mile. You will pass your first junction on your right, followed by a set of power lines overhead and then a second junction on your right. Continue ahead until you reach the third junction on your right. It is easily marked with a bench and a memorial plaque. From here, turn right into the woods and continue ahead.

It is important if you are unfamiliar with these woods that you do not deviate from these directions. The woods are large and dense and have many trails running through them, which makes it easy to get lost and lose your bearings.

9 After 300m into the woods you meet a crossroads, turn left.

10 At the next grassy crossroads, continue ahead.

11 At the third crossroads, turn left.

12 Continue along this path. Where the path forks, bear left.

13 At the next T-junction, turn left.

14 After 100m, you will meet another crossroads with a bench on your right. At this crossroads, turn right.

15 At the final crossroads, continue ahead. You will notice that you are on the edge of the wood. Follow this path round until you meet a metal gate. Go through the gate and turn left on to the track which after 100m leads you back to the car park.

Exploring the wood.

3

Twigmoor Woods

Dogs will enjoy a swim at Gull Ponds.

This stunning wood in North Lincolnshire is one of the most beautiful to explore and will be especially loved by children. It has a main path around the wood, and many different trails leading off it. Take your compass and don't be afraid to check out these paths because it really is worth being adventurous and your dog will love it. On the way round you come across a beautiful lake, ideal for dogs to swim in. Or for a lovely picnic spot follow the directions to the secluded pond. A lovely year round adventure that will have you returning time and time again.

Lincolnshire – A Dog Walker's Guide

Terrain

Definitely a wellie walk. Although the main track through the woods is good, tracks leading off can be muddy after wet weather. The main track is flat, however, there are some inclines off the main track.

Where to park

There is a signed and free car park at Twigmoor Woods. **OS map:** Explorer 281 Ancholme Valley (GR: SE 944 058)

How to get there

Twigmoor Woods is right at the end of the A15. It can be reached from the A15, by turning off at Gainsthorpe and Cleatham just north of Kirton in Lindsey. Drive through Gainsthorpe to a crossroads and turn right onto B1398. Follow this road past Greetwell and the wood is signposted on your left. Otherwise, from A18, turn off for the B1398 towards Greetwell.

Nearest refreshments

The Sutton Arms, West St, Scawby, DN20 9AN and The Wheatsheaf, Station Rd, Hibaldstow, DN20 9EB are the nearest country pubs to Twigmoor Woods. They both offer a friendly service and food although dogs are not allowed inside during food service time.

The Walk

● ●

1 From the car park, turn on to the main woodland path by the information board and walk straight ahead for a while. As the path branches off to the right, you continue ahead and walk downhill towards a wooden bench.

2 By the bench, turn left on to a small woodland path and follow it. When you reach a Y-junction, turn left, following the path uphill and at the top, you go

Dog factors

Distance: 2¾ miles.
Road Walking: None.
Livestock: None.
Stiles: None.
Nearest Vets: Ashby Road Veterinary Surgery, 287 Ashby Road, Scunthorpe DN16 2AB ☎ 01724 842 655

back downhill and continue ahead. Steadily climb another hill until you reach the top. Here is a newly planted area. Go towards a grassy triangular junction and turn right.

③ Follow the path through ferns as it weaves downhill through the woods amidst stunning scenery. Continue to follow the path ahead, do not stray off it. Eventually, you reach a small pond area on your right. Cross the pond between two trees where the water is shallowest and go up the bank on to the other side. Follow this path which may have some shallow pond-like areas to cross after wet weather.

④ At the end of this path you meet the main track. Turn left and follow this track until you reach a crossroads by a wooden signpost. Turn left and continue along a grassy bank. (This area can be damp underfoot after wet weather.) After 500m you meet a wooden signpost where the path bears right. Continue ahead to the end, where it bears right by the signpost and carry on following the **circular walk** sign on the main path.

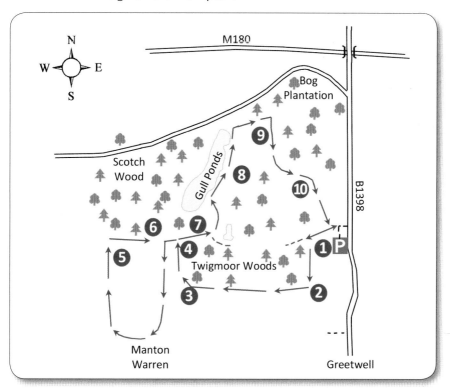

5 At the end of this path, it bears right towards a crossroads. Turn right and follow the sign for the **car park**.

6 At the next crossroads, continue ahead past the wooden signpost.

7 After a short while you reach a junction on your left which is not marked, but it is part of the main track through the woods. Take this turning and follow it for around 400m until you see a path through an opening on your right beside a pond. This path just leads to a secluded pond which makes a lovely picnic spot.

8 Back on the main track, you continue ahead until you reach a T-junction by a bench. Turn left and as you walk along you will see **Gull Ponds**, a real treat for your dog.

9 Continue ahead from Gull Ponds back on the main track. The path bears left and you follow it round. After 100m, you will see a path into the woods through ferns on your right. Take this path into the woods.

10 Follow this woodland path and bear left after 100m, where you will see a wooden footbridge in the distance. Continue past the footbridge and follow the path that leads to a second footbridge. Continue past this until you rejoin the main track. Turn right on the main track and follow this track back to the car park.

Pretty picnic spot by the secluded pond.

4

Nettleton Valley

Taking a break.

When **exploring this area**, you may be forgiven for thinking you are no longer in Lincolnshire. With its rolling hills and captivating valleys, this walk takes you close to the highest peak in Lincolnshire. It begins by climbing grazing fields and crossing this stunning peaceful landscape. Before reaching a quiet country road with majestic views stretching for miles all the way back. Your dog will enjoy the freedom of bounding across the fields, but remember that he will have to share some of them with livestock.

Lincolnshire – A Dog Walker's Guide

Terrain
Hilly in places. Can be muddy underfoot in some fields after wet weather.

Where to Park
There is a free car park marked on the map, ¾ mile south of Nettleton. **OS map:** Explorer 284 Grimsby, Cleethorpes and Immingham (GR: TF 111 991).

How to get there
From the A46 approaching Nettleton, take the turn signposted 'Nettleton & Normandy', by the Salutation Inn public house. Pass the church on your left and bear right passing Wold Farm. Keep bearing right until you leave the village. After ¾ mile on your right is the car park.

Nearest refreshments
Hope Tavern at Holton Le Moor, LN7 6AH is a 19th-century inn sitting beside the railway. It has a pretty beer garden, log fire and serves food.

    The nearest pub is The Salutation Inn in Nettleton LN7 6NP. It has a beer garden and serves food. Dogs are allowed inside out of food service times.

The Walk
. . . .

1 Turn left out of the car park and walk down the lane towards the village signed Nettleton. Continue through the village until the road forks beside Old White Cottage. Here there is a **Viking Way** marker and you turn right on to a track.

2 Follow the track for about ¼ mile towards an equestrian centre at Nettleton Grange. At the public bridleway sign, turn left, walking up towards the metal gate and turn right onto the **Viking Way**. The hedge line should be on your

Dog factors
. . . .
Distance: 4½ miles.
Road Walking: Walk down a quiet country lane at the end of the walk.
Livestock: Yes, grazing cows.
Stiles: None.
Nearest Vets: Marshlands Veterinary Centre, Unit 1, Enterprise Park, Priory Road, Boston PE22 0JZ ☎ 01205 760587

right and you approach a pond. Walk towards the posts in the field which are markers for the Viking Way. Cross a wooden bridge and climb the bank towards the next marked post while you continue to follow the contours of the valley.

❸ You now cross a bridge towards two field boundaries and continue ahead until you reach the end of the field. Cross the cattle bridge and continue ahead. At the end of the field you cross a wooden bridge with a metal gate and continue ahead. Pass a wooden footpath with the metal gate. Here you will see your first yellow warning sign regarding livestock. Continue ahead and cross the field leaving through a metal gate at the end.

❹ Turn left and walk up the track where there is a bench for a rest stop. Half way up the hill is a public footpath signpost where you turn right and walk downhill through the wooded area.

❺ Once you leave the wooded area you meet two metal gates in a field. Walk along the right side of the field edge until you reach the end where there are another two metal gates leading you into the next field. Follow the line of the telegraph poles, staying low, and then veer right at the end of the field towards the gate in the far right corner.

❻ You now leave the field and begin to follow a track alongside an arable field. At the end of the track you

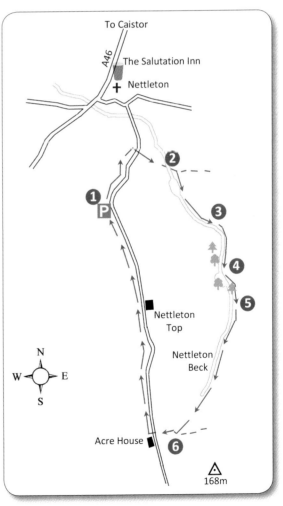

meet a T-junction with a country road beside Acre House. Turn right and follow this path back down to the car park. The verges are wide on this very quiet road and the views all around are stunning. A well behaved dog would not need to be on a lead on this stretch until you reach the final steep descent just beside the car park where the verges narrow.

Note:
The Nettleton valley is a beautiful and striking area. It unavoidably has livestock in some of its fields and there are yellow warning signs for walkers advising them to take care when crossing fields. Generally, the animals (cows and bulls) are quiet and will ignore walkers, but can be distracted by a dog or become protective if they have calves with them. The fields you cross are vast, and the cattle tend to congregate away from footpaths, so please heed the warning and do not be put off exploring this beautiful area.

Stunning views over Lincolnshire's highest point.

5

Saltfleetby-Theddlethorpe Nature Reserve

Stunning coastal walks.

You can't beat a leisurely stroll along the beach. Dogs love the freedom and the fresh Lincolnshire sea air blowing through their ears! This walk gathers the delights of Saltfleetby-Theddlethorpe Dunes Nature Reserve, taking in a walk along the long sandy beach and past the sand dunes. It then wanders out into the lovely countryside before rejoining the nature reserve.

Terrain

Good all weather walk. Uneven in places.

Where to park

The nature reserve has a free car park at Rimac near Saltfleetby St Clement on the corner of A1031. **OS map:** 283 Explorer Louth & Mablethorpe. (GR: TF 467 917/Sat Nav: LN11 7TR)

How to get there

Take the A1031 from Mablethorpe. As you approach the T-junction for Saltfleetby All Saints, turn right, following the A1031 for a short distance before approaching a sharp left bend. On the bend you turn off for the Rimac car park and nature reserve. Follow this track down to the car park.

Nearest refreshments

En route is The Crown Inn at Saltfleet with its lovely beer garden. You also pass the very good Seawaves Fish & Chips shop as you walk through the caravan park. For a real treat at the end of your walk, try The Kings Head at Theddlethorpe, LN12 1PB. This beautiful thatched cottage pub has a beer garden and is very dog friendly inside and out.

The Walk

. . . .

1 From the **Rimac car park**, walk towards the noticeboard and through the gate, bearing left on to the footpath. Continue ahead towards a wooden gate by a tide warning sign. Go through the gate on to a grassy path and walk towards the marshes before turning left by a post with a blue arrow.

2 You now follow this clear track along the edge of the marshes. You will pass the **Sea View Farm car park** on your left and also a disused Second World

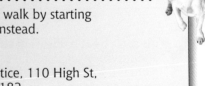

Dog factors

. . . .

Distance: 5 miles. You can shorten this walk by starting and ending at Sea View Farm car park instead.
Livestock: None.
Stiles: 1.
Nearest Vets: Fenwold Veterinary Practice, 110 High St, Mablethorpe LN12 1BG ☎ 01507 478182

War pillbox on your right as you continue ahead towards the end of this stretch, marked by a bridge crossing the **Great Eau**.

❸ Cross the bridge, following the track straight ahead until you meet a main road (A1031). Turn right and walk to the next footpath sign which is 80m away, where you turn right at the **Saltfleet Haven** sign. Follow the track, past the sewage works all the way to the end where there is a small car park. At the back of the car park, go up the steps and pick up one of the faint paths through the dunes.

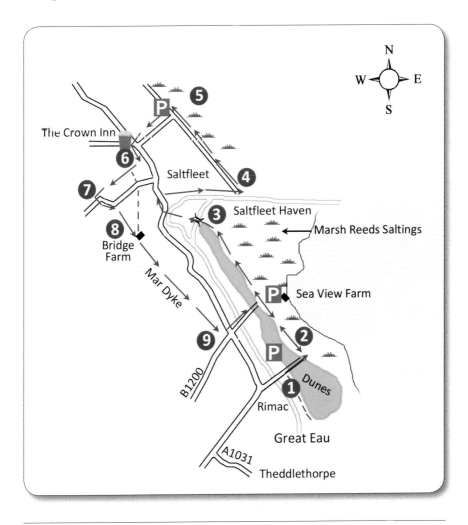

Walking in the nature reserve.

4 Now heading in a north-westerly direction along the dunes, you follow this path for ½ mile. There is a picnic table on your left if you fancy a rest. Alternatively, you could walk down to the water's edge from this point, but expect to add another 30 minutes to your walk when the tide is out.

5 Continue ahead until you reach a steep concrete ramp by a flag pole, marked with a **Humber Estuary European Marine** sign. Turn left here, leaving the dunes. You now begin to walk down Sea Lane beside a caravan park. Halfway down is **Seawaves fish and chips shop** with outdoor seating if you fancy a bite.

6 Continue right to the end towards the main road. Turn left and cross over towards **The Crown Inn**. Turn right down **Pump Lane** and follow the road all the way down, bearing left at the bottom of the lane towards a public footpath sign. Cross the wooden footbridge into a playing field and walk directly ahead, crossing the field towards another wooden footbridge beside the black bin.

7 From the wooden footbridge, walk along the grassy footpath all the way to the end until you meet another public footpath sign. Here you emerge on to the bend of **Louth Road**. Turn left on to the road and continue for approx. 300m to the next public footpath sign which approaches on your right. Enter the arable field here and follow the long field-edge footpath ahead by **Hill Top Farm**.

8 At the end of the field you meet a public footpath sign. Continue over the small wooden bridge and follow the markers into the next field. Cross another bridge and begin to walk alongside **Mar Dike drain**.

At the end of **Mar Dike drain**, you cross a wooden footbridge towards a section of field (with livestock fenced off) for about 100m until you reach the stile.

9 Cross the stile, turn left on to the road and walk towards the crossroads. Go straight over the crossroads and continue down the lane towards **Sea View Farm car park**. You are now retracing your steps back to the car park. Turn right on the footpath by a white barrier and follow the footpath until you reach a wooden gate. Continue ahead, following the field edge. At the end is a wooden gate, leading you back to your start point at the **Rimac car park**.

6

Burwell and Muckton Woods

Looking across Burwell Wood.

This beautiful hilltop area enjoys stunning open views across the countryside. Skirting the edge of Burwell Wood, you can enjoy the tranquillity of this bracing ramble alongside arable fields. This walk can be enjoyed year round, but is particularly beautiful in summer when the fields are at their most golden, with clear paths marking the rights of way through them. The arable fields make this particularly appealing for dogs to roam, as does the chance to explore woodland.

Terrain
Hilly and uneven in places. Can be muddy underfoot in some sections.

Where to park
The lay-by beside the A16 in Burwell outside the 12th-century St Michael's church and near The Stags Head Inn **OS map:** Explorer 283 Louth & Mablethorpe (GR: TF 355 796/Sat Nav: LN11 8PR).

How to get there
Take the A16 Louth to Boston road. Burwell is 4 miles south of Louth.

Nearest refreshments
The Stags Head Inn in Burwell LN11 8PR is close to the parking lay-by, but is not open all day. The Royal Oak Inn or 'The Splash' as it is locally known, at Little Cawthorpe LN11 8LZ is a lovely 17th-century traditional pub serving good food. Dogs are allowed in the beer garden.

The Walk

1 From the parking bay outside the church, walk towards the **Stags Head Inn**, where there is a public footpath signpost just before it. Turn left here and walk beside an octagonal building. The path leads you up a hill, passing the graveyard of the redundant **St Michael's church** on your left.

2 At the top of the hill, continue straight across the arable field on a right of way path. (This is much easier to see when the crops are growing). At the end of the field, bear left on to the track and towards the public footpath sign. At the signpost, turn right on to the grassy track which is **Crab Tree Walk Plantation**. Continue to follow this track for ¾ mile until you reach the edge of **Burwell Wood**.

Dog factors

Distance: 6 miles.
Road Walking: Short walk on a country lane.
Livestock: There are cattle at point 5.
Stiles: 2.
Nearest Vets: Rase Veterinary Centre, 17 Newmarket, Louth LN11 9HH ☎ 01507 607718

3 There is a public footpath sign at the end of the plantation walk. From here, enter **Burwell Wood** straight ahead, descending some steps. Follow the woodland path until it brings you out to a track by another public footpath sign. Turn left, follow the track for 15m before turning right by the yellow way-marker. You now begin to walk along the wood edge with open views across the countryside.

4 At the end of the path you reach a large log (makes a pleasant rest stop), cross a short track through Burwell Wood and through a metal gate, following the yellow way-markers. Continue ahead.

5 Follow the wood edge until you reach the next public footpath sign. Here you have right of way to cross the arable field to the other side where there is a stile. Put your dog on a lead before entering the field as there might be cattle here. Stay to the far right of the field for the short walk

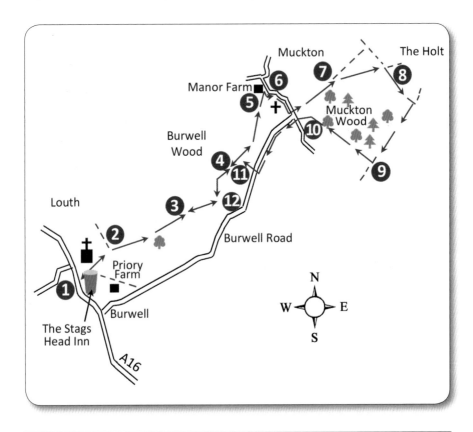

to the stile at the other side. It can be very muddy around the stile. As you leave the field, you pass a white house and walk down the farm track of **Manor Farm**.

⑥ You are now entering **Muckton** and walk down to the country road. Turn right, walk through the village passing a small church and red telephone box on your right. When you reach the T-junction for **Alford & Aby**, turn left down the track marked with a public footpath and bridleway signpost.

⑦ Continue to follow this track down, where you will see **Muckton Wood** on your right. As you follow the track for a while, you will reach a public footpath sign. Turn right here, crossing the field diagonally as you head towards **The Holt**. There is a wooden footbridge at the end. Cross the second field and take the wooden footbridge into **The Holt**.

⑧ Turn right and follow the path that weaves through the wood until it comes out on to a track by a public footpath sign. Turn right and follow the track until it leaves the wood. You now reach a public bridleway sign and turn right. Continue to follow this grassy path towards Muckton Wood, with the hedge line on your right. Muckton Wood is marked by a way-marker as you enter it. Follow the path, which passes a fence inside the wood. The wood is owned by Lincolnshire Wildlife Trust with access only along the wood edge.

⑨ As you leave Muckton Wood, you meet a way-marker and turn right, following the wood edge beside an arable field. Half way down, you meet a track. Cross it and continue until you reach the far corner of the wood by a way-marker. You have right of way to cross the arable field diagonally, back towards the track.

⑩ As you reach the track, turn left, back onto the road by the junction. Cross the road and follow the signpost left for Burwell. You now walk along a quiet country road which steadily climbs uphill. As you reach the top of the hill you will see a private gated wood on your right marked **Harrison Woodlands Haugham & Burwell**. Continue for another 10m until you turn right into the field alongside it. Walk alongside the wood edge towards the top of the field. You are now beginning to retrace your steps when you see the big log on your right in the field corner. Turn left, follow the field edge with Burwell Wood on your right.

⑪ At the end of the field, turn left by a way-marker into the woods and after 15m turn right on to the woodland path, climbing up the wooden steps which lead you out of the wood.

12 As you clear Burwell Wood, you begin to walk back along **Crab Tree Walk Plantation** for ¾ mile. At the end of the plantation walk, you meet a public footpath sign. Turn left, and then right after 20m by the way-marker. Walk back across the field towards the church. You now finish with your final descent down the hill beside the graveyard, back towards your start point.

Note:
This is a long walk which can be easily split into two separate walks if required.
Walk 1: Burwell Wood.
Follow points 1 to 6, then 10 to 12, where you leave Muckton and turn back towards Burwell.

Walk 2: The Holt and Muckton Wood.
Park outside Muckton, opposite the signposted T-junction. There is off-road parking on the track. Follow points 7 to 10.

There are warning signs on this section of the walk to keep dogs on leads. This is due to pest control chemicals being used in the area, particularly around Muckton Wood Nature Reserve. If you have a dog who likes to forage, bear this in mind.

Walking along Crab Tree Walk Plantation in autumn.

Saltfleetby-Theddlethorpe Dunes

Space to run and play.

Dogs just love a day out at the seaside! During high season, it's difficult to find a beach which is both pleasant to walk on and dog friendly – Saltfleetby-Theddlethorpe Dunes Nature Reserve is both. It offers one of the best coastal walks in Lincolnshire and a trip to the seaside at any time of the year is a joy. It's a popular spot with local dog walkers so there'll be some sniffing and greeting for your pet. The beach is both stunning and peaceful and this simple walk makes the most of this beautiful coastline.

Terrain

Good all weather, all year walk. Flat, sandy terrain.

Where to Park

There are several car parks along the stretch of coastline at Saltfleetby-Theddlethorpe Dunes National Nature Reserve. Most are not marked from the road. This walk starts at the free Churchill Lane car park. **OS map:** Explorer 283 Louth & Mablethorpe (GR: TA 478 901).

How to get there

From the A1031, coming from Mablethorpe, you drive past the gas works towards Theddlethorpe St Helen. Pass GT motors on your right, then a church almost immediately afterwards, before reaching a sharp right bend in the road. You head down a straight section of road before a sharp left turn by a signpost for Grimsby and Louth. Instead of following the bend round, turn down Churchill Lane immediately ahead, and follow the lane to the bottom, where you will see the car park.

Nearest refreshments

The Kings Head Inn at Theddlethorpe, LN12 1PB, is a beautiful and unique thatched cottage pub with a lovely beer garden, which is very dog friendly inside and out. ☎ 01507 339798

Mablethorpe seafront has lots of choice for food and drink in this small seaside town and is worth a visit. The Clock fish & chips restaurant on Seaholme Road is one of the best in town.

The Walk

. . . .

1 From **Churchill Lane car park**, walk towards the noticeboard beside the

Dog factors

. . . .

Distance: 3 miles.
Road Walking: None.
Livestock: None.
Stiles: None.
Nearest Vets: Fenwold Veterinary Practice, 110 High St,
Mablethorpe LN12 1BG ☎ 01507 478182

white barrier. Walk around the barrier and follow this path for about 300m until it reaches the beach. As you walk on to the beach you will see a **white flag pole** where you turn right and walk down the beach for ¾ mile until you pass the first car park. The first car park is **Brickyard Lane** and is marked with a tall wooden post with a red rhombus shaped sign. Continue to walk along the beach.

2 After another ¾ mile, you meet **Crook Bank car park**. You will see a clear opening in the dunes, as the sand becomes a lane, marked with tide warning boards. Turn right here and follow the lane towards the car park.

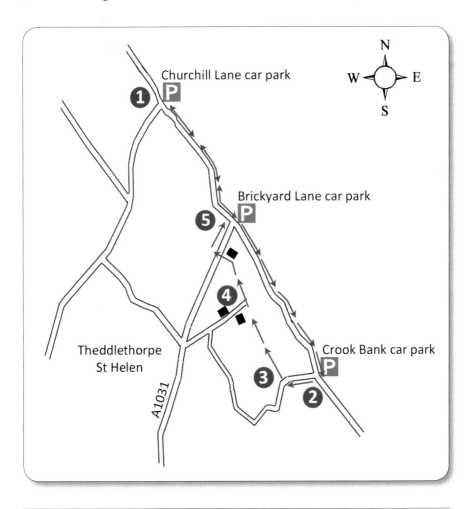

Lincolnshire – A Dog Walker's Guide

3 Bypass the car park on your right and follow the bendy lane for a short while until you see a public footpath sign on the bend. Turn right here and walk along the edge of an arable field towards **Pear Tree Farm**. At the end of the field, you pass a farmhouse on your left. Bear right off the track by a public footpath sign and continue across the field edge.

4 As you reach the next farmhouse, bear left immediately beside it where there is a yellow way-marker. Walk along the very narrow path towards a wooden trestle gate. Turn left and follow the track to a gated entrance.

5 As you reach **Brickyard Lane**, turn right and follow the road to the end, marked by two white cottages and **Brickyard Lane car park**. Continue along the track, past the metal barrier and towards the beach. Once at the beach, turn left and continue back for ¾ mile towards **Churchill Lane car park**. It is marked with a white flag pole and also a wooden post with a red warning sign.

If you want to add to your walk, take time to walk your dog out to the sea. When the tide is out, it can take about 30 minutes for a return walk.

Nice to be beside the seaside.

Chambers Farm Wood
(near Wragby)

Dogs always love exploring the woods.

Chambers Farm Wood is a gem in the crown of the Lincolnshire Wolds. Part of the Bardney Limewoods Nature Reserve, it has easy marked trails to follow on good paths, making it excellent as a year-round walk. There are picnic tables to rest at and a beautiful dedicated butterfly garden to explore. There is also a meadow called Little Scrubs to attract butterflies. It has three main trails and we cover two in this walk which are great introductions to this stunning area. Dogs will love exploring the winding paths and sniffing in the undergrowth.

Lincolnshire – A Dog Walker's Guide

Terrain

Flat, even terrain. Well maintained paths. Some paths away from the surfaced trail can be muddy underfoot.

Where to Park

Car park at Chambers Farm Wood. **OS Map:** Explorer 273 Lincolnshire Wolds South (GR: TF 148 738).

How to get there

From the B1202 Wragby-Bardney road, the wood is signposted with brown tourist signs after leaving Bardney.

Nearest refreshments

The Riverside Inn, Southrey. LN3 5TA is dog friendly, has a lovely beer garden and is open all day ☎ 01526 398374. The Ivy, Market Place Wragby, LN8 5QU is a 17th-century inn where dogs are allowed in the beer garden ☎ 01673 858768.

The Walk

❶ This walk begins from the car park. Walk away from the car barrier, until you see a small opening in the woods with a white tipped post. Turn left at the first post and begin to follow the surfaced path through the woods. This is a very simple trail to follow and it takes you to the end where the path curves to the right. As you follow it round, there is a notice on your left guiding you towards **Little Scrubbs**, a butterfly meadow, stunning in spring and summer. You can either take this semi-circular path through the meadow or continue ahead.

Dog factors

Distance: 3¼ miles.
Road Walking: None.
Livestock: None.
Stiles: None.
Nearest Vets: Orchard House Veterinary Surgery, 8 Prince's Street, Metheringham, LN4 3BX ☎ 01526 320387
Also: Lincs Veterinary Solutions Ltd, Old Market Place Stores, Market Place, Wragby LN8 5QU ☎ 01673 857849

2 At the end you pass a bench and follow the path to the right as it weaves through the woods. There are plenty of benches and wooden animal sculptures en route. Continue to follow this path all the way round until it makes a sharp left turn by a white tipped post.

3 Follow the path towards the next white tipped post where the path makes a Y-junction. Take the smaller path into the woods, directly ahead and follow the thin trail. It can be muddy underfoot on this section.

4 At the end of this path you meet the main surfaced trail, The Red Trail. Turn left onto this path. This is a flat path and very easy to follow. The first section is straight, with forest lining the sides of the path. Keep ahead, then bear left. The walk then takes a more interesting and enclosed appearance.

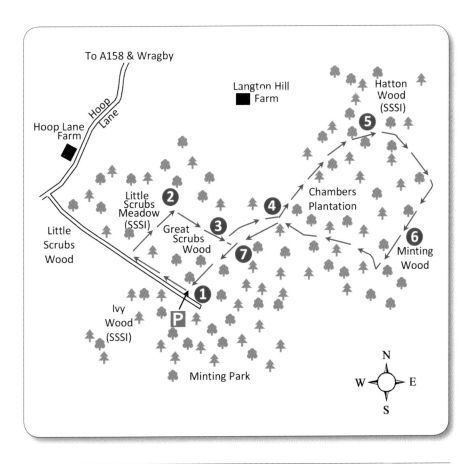

5 Follow the path as it eventually curves around towards Hatton Woods, which is home to rare barbastelle bats. You will notice another path leading left. Ignore it, unless you are feeling adventurous and want to explore deeper inside these pretty woods. To stay on the **Red Trail**, you will see a red marker ahead leading you right.

6 You now walk alongside **Minting Wood**, again a home to bats. This path takes you back to the earlier Y-junction. Head left and follow the red markers.

7 Once you reach the first white-tipped post, turn right, back into the woods and follow the path all the way round to the next post on a bend beside an opening into the woods. Go through the opening. This is known as **The Dog Walkers' Path**, and takes you through the enclosed wood, away from paths. It can be muddy underfoot in here. Follow this all the way through the wood until you reach the car park at the end.

Beautiful autumn walks.

Skellingthorpe Old Wood

Heading into the woods.

Skellingthorpe Old Wood sits on the edge of Lincoln. It requires a long stroll up to it from the village as it does not have any parking areas, but this can be incorporated into a lovely walk in areas you would not normally have passed through. The wood itself has many trails running through it and is worth coming back to again and again to explore the different paths. Your dog will love the freedom of roaming through the woods.

Lincolnshire – A Dog Walker's Guide

Terrain

Flat even terrain. Can be muddy underfoot on some woodland trails after wet weather.

Where to park

There is the large Community Centre car park in Skellingthorpe village. It is well signposted. **OS map:** Explorer 272 Lincoln (GR: SK 926 716/Sat Nav: LN6 5UT).

How to get there

From the A46 Newark to Lincoln road, turn off at the roundabout (Skellingthorpe & Birchwood) for Skellingthorpe, just outside Lincoln.

Nearest refreshments

The Plough Inn on the High Street in Skellingthorpe has a beer garden and also welcomes dogs indoors. This pub does not serve food, but is open all day. For something different, try the Daisy Made café and ice-cream parlour (which is also a drive-in) in Skellingthorpe. It has animal pens and plenty to keep children entertained. Dogs are allowed outside by the picnic benches.

The Walk

1 From the **community centre**, walk to the rear of the car park. Just before you reach the play area, turn left on to the path. This is part of a cycle track. Continue ahead.

2 Continue across the crossroads, and on reaching the bridge, continue under

Dog factors

Distance: 4¼ miles.
Road walking: Walk along a country lane and through the village.
Livestock: None. This is an equestrian area and you may pass some horse-riders on the bridleway.
Stiles: None.
Nearest vets: Lincvet, Unit 21, Birchwood Shopping Centre, Jasmin Road, Lincoln LN6 0QQ ☎ 01522 694 275

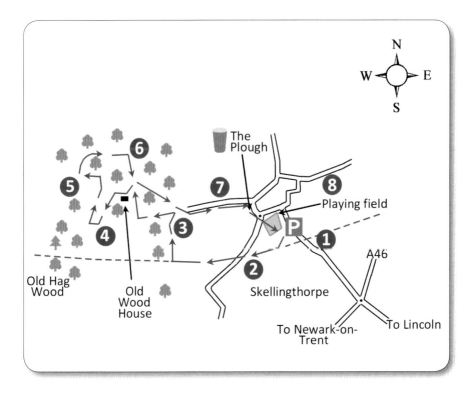

it, bearing left after the bridge by the **signpost (no.64)** and follow the track. Stay on the track for a while until you see a 'restricted byway' sign on both sides. Turn right here, into the woods and continue to follow the path which opens up into a track and passes some houses and equestrian fields.

3 At the end of the track, you cross a small bridge by **Old Wood Nursery** and turn left at the public bridleway sign. Continue to follow the track. You pass some houses on your left with a stream running alongside. Follow the track until you reach a signpost. Turn right into the woods on to a restricted byway. At the end of this track you meet a crossroads by a **Woodland Trust** sign. Turn left and follow the path which leads towards **Old Wood House**. Bear right, following the path.

4 At the end of the path is a metal gate and a wooden fence. Walk through the gap in the fence with a way-marker bearing left (not the metal gate), and follow the path that bears left into the woods. This path continues up

Lots of paths to explore.

towards the edge of the woods and comes out on to the main track by a public bridleway sign. Turn right and follow the path along the edge of the woods. It can be muddy underfoot in this section. When you reach the next junction, continue ahead. At the next T-junction, turn right. Continue ahead past the next T-junction. At the next T-junction, turn left as this takes you past an S-bend and up a tree-lined avenue towards a bench at a crossroads. Turn right here.

5 Follow the path through the woods, which can be muddy underfoot. At the end is a gate and fence, leaving behind an **Old Wood – Welcome** sign.

6 Turn right and follow the track down towards a crossroads by a signpost with multiple choices. Take the second junction (ahead) on to the road, and walk past a number of houses until reaching the road junction at the end. Bear left and continue to follow the road to the village for a short distance.

7 As you reach the village you pass **Woodbank Cemetery** on your left. Continue ahead towards the bridge and past **Old Chapel Road**. At the T-junction, turn right down the **High Street**, crossing a bridge as you approach **The Plough** village pub.

8 Continue past The Plough towards the Co-op. At the Co-op, turn right at the Give Way sign and cross the road towards the park and public footpath sign on **Jerusalem Road**. Walk across the playing field, alongside the play area then turn left into the car park.

Southrey Wood and Tupholme Abbey

Crossing the cornfields.

My dogs find this walk a complete adventure with its long grass and varied tracks. It starts by the edge of the river Witham and heads up to Southrey Wood, part of the Bardney Limewoods Nature Reserve. The Lincolnshire Wolds are known for their beauty and this walk also takes you along arable farmland and past the ruins of the 12th-century Tupholme Abbey, before arriving back at the Riverside Inn for refreshments. In the summer, these fields are awash with golden corn.

Terrain

Good all weather walk on flat, even terrain. Can be muddy underfoot in some sections of the wood or when crossing the field footpaths in winter.

Where to park

Free car park at the end of Ferry Road beside the Riverside Inn. **OS map:** Explorer 273 Lincolnshire Wolds South (GR: TF 138 664/Sat Nav: LN3 5TA).

How to get there

From Bardney, follow the B1190 for Southrey, passing the cemetery and allotments on your left. Follow the road as it passes Southrey Wood on your right. Where the road begins to fork, bear right, following signs to Southrey. This is Ferry Road, remain on it through the village, past the Riverside Inn, and towards the car park right at the end of the road.

Nearest refreshments

The Riverside Inn, Southrey LN3 5TA is dog friendly with a lovely beer garden and open all day. There are also several pubs in Bardney village.

The Walk

. . . .

1 From the car park, turn towards the **Riverside Inn** and walk down the road through the village. Pass **Lowthorpe** and **St John the Divine church** on your right. Turn left into **Highthorpe**, which puts you on The Viking Way. Continue through the village, passing the village hall on your right.

Dog factors
. . . .
Distance: 5¼ miles.
Road walking: A short walk through the village and cross the B1190.
Livestock: A horse and a 200m walk through a field of cows.
Stiles: 2.
Nearest Vets: Orchard House Veterinary Surgery, 8 Prince's Street, Metheringham, LN4 3BX ☎ 01526 320387

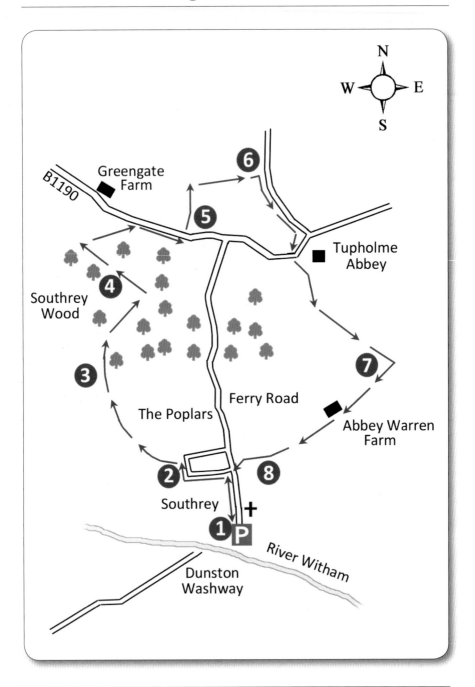

2 At the end of the village, the road bears round to the right. Continue ahead along this quiet lane towards the junction marked 'public bridleway to Southrey Wood'. Here, turn left, passing **Poplar Farm** and following the track. Where the track curves to the right, continue on it towards the wood.

3 At the end of the track is a public bridleway sign. Turn right, and begin to skirt the edge of **Southrey Wood**. After 100m, there is an unmarked opening into the woods. Go into the wood and turn immediately left, following the well trodden footpath which parallels the edge of the wood. At the first fork, bear right, taking you deeper into the woods.

Continue to walk through the woods, which have a few watering holes for your dog. As you reach the end of the wood, the path becomes a track. Once outside there is a turning area on your right, continue past this. After 20m take the unmarked opening back into the woods on your left.

4 Follow the path through this very pretty part of the woods. You will reach a hide at a crossroads where you continue ahead towards the edge of the woods. Here you meet a T-junction where you turn right.

As you leave the wood enclosure, you pass **Greengate Farm** and equestrian field on your left. Continue ahead towards the road but just before you meet the road, bear right, going straight back into the woods. (You do not need to walk on the road). You should now be walking parallel to the road through the woods. Continue along the footpath until you meet a Forestry Commission sign for **Southrey Wood** on your right. Continue to walk by the edge of the woods until you reach the next track with the sign 'no admittance to unauthorised vehicles'. *From here you can take a shorter option and follow the 1¼ mile signpost back to the village if you wish.*

5 Turn left and cross the road into an arable field by a public bridleway sign. Continue ahead with the hedge line on your left. At the end of this field, you meet another field with a yellow way-marker. Bear left, continuing with the hedge line on your left. At the public bridleway sign, turn right and continue ahead. As you reach the end of this field there is a small wooden footbridge to cross into the next field and you continue ahead.

At the end of this field, cross the stile into the paddock, which may have a horse in it, so dogs on leads. Walk from the stile, past the gate, to the far right edge of the paddock towards the second stile.

6 You are now beside **Low Road Farm** in Tupholme. Walk to the track and turn right. Follow this quiet track all the way down until you meet the B1190 road at a T-junction. Turn right, following the road for 200m until you meet the sign for **Tupholme Abbey**. Cross the road towards the abbey and go through the metal gate.

Keep your dog on a lead if you decide to explore the ruins, as grazing livestock roam here. Otherwise, stay on the track by the public bridleway sign and continue along this grassy track for approx 1 mile.

7 At the end of the track, turn right on to The Viking Way by the markers. Continue to walk towards **Abbey Warren Farm** where there's a metal gate and a field of cows. Ensure you close the gate securely behind you and put your dog on a lead. Now cross the field for a short distance, passing a pond on your right, and directly through the metal gate at the other side. Close the gate securely. *Remember, when passing cows with a dog walk briskly and quietly. Keep as far away from the cows as possible and if you feel threatened, let your dog off the lead as he will be able to outrun the cows.*

8 Continue ahead on a grassy track until you reach the next field, accessed by crossing a wooden footbridge. Here you see the signpost for 'Southrey ¼ mile'. Continue across the field towards the village. At the end of the field, turn left and walk 500m back to the Riverside Inn and car park.

Resting in the meadows.

Nocton Wood and the Wolds

Peaceful tracks and plenty of space.

Your dog will love splashing in the streams that skirt the woods in this pretty, peaceful part of the Wolds. This lovely walk skirts the edge of privately-owned Nocton Wood in the Lincolnshire Wolds. The well-laid tracks make it an excellent all weather walk and a chance to ramble across arable farmland and country lanes.

Lincolnshire – A Dog Walker's Guide

Terrain
Good all weather walk on flat, even tracks.

Where to park
Free walkers' car park beside Nocton Wood. **OS map:** Explorer 272 Lincoln (GR: TF 089 638).

How to get there
From the B1188 Ruskington to Lincoln road, turn off at Dunston village and follow the brown tourist signs 'Stepping Out'. Continue to follow the Stepping Out signs through the village to Dunston Fen Lane. This country road follows the edge of the wood and eventually bears left, where there is a sign for the car park. Picnic tables and benches are on site.

Nearest refreshments
The Red Lion Pub, Dunston LN4 2EW is a typical country pub serving good food in a pleasant setting. Dogs are not allowed inside, but are allowed in the lovely beer garden. The White Horse Inn near Southrey, LN4 3AP is 2½ miles up Dunston Fen Lane from the car park. It sits on the banks of the river Witham in a pleasant setting. Dogs are welcome in the front and back beer gardens.

The Walk

● ●

1 Leaving the car park area, turn left and follow the track with the wood on your left-hand side. Along this section runs a stream of clean water for your dog to enjoy. You then reach **Nocton Delph Head Bridge**, continuing along the track until you approach a road on the corner of **Wasps Nest**.

Dog factors
● ●

Distance: 3 miles.
Road walking: A section of very quiet country road on Dunston Fen Lane at the end of the walk. Verges are wide, so well-behaved dogs will be fine off the lead.
Livestock: None.
Stiles: None.
Nearest Vets: Orchard House Veterinary Surgery, 8 Prince's Street, Metheringham, LN4 3BX ☎ 01526 320387

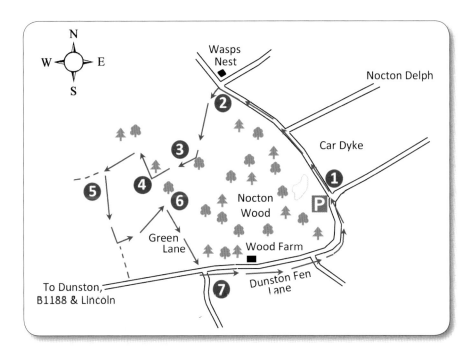

② At **Wasps Nest**, turn left, crossing a small bridge towards a public bridleway sign that bears left. Walk up the track towards Nocton Wood and after a short distance, you will be walking alongside the edge of the wood.

③ At the top of the track you meet a gate, where you turn off the track by the public bridleway sign on to a grassy path that leads you between two fields. As you continue along this pretty stretch of walk, you reach a bench on a bend by a copse of trees. Continue along the track all the way to the end, passing a shelter on your left.

④ At the junction, by a restricted byway sign, turn right and continue to the end of this track. Turn left at the T-junction. Follow the lane down where you can see Nocton Hall in the distance on your right.

⑤ When you reach a crossroads by a gated drive, turn left on to the public bridleway and follow the track across a field, with the hedgerow on your left. Continue ahead, passing a pubic bridleway sign. After another 200m, you meet a public footpath sign. Turn left, leaving the track and crossing between two fields towards the wood.

6 As you reach the edge of the wood, turn right by the restricted byway sign for **Green Lane**. Follow the line of telegraph poles on your left down the edge of the wood until you reach a road. Here you meet **Prior Lane** and turn left towards the Dunston Fen and Metheringham Fen signpost.

7 Continue along this quiet road section. Just after passing **Wood Farm Lodge**, you see a section of stream on your left, which is ideal clean water for your dog, but does have a current. Follow the road section for ½ mile. You will see a Stepping Out sign on your left, taking you back to the car park.

Enjoying the sunshine!

Ostler's Plantation and the Dambusters

Walking by the heathland.

Ostler's Plantation was once an airfield used by the Dambusters squadron in the Second World War. As you wander through the lush woodlands, evidence of its past still remain, with taxiways and bunkers at various turns. Many paths weave through the woodland, while others follow the edge of Kirkby Moor Nature Reserve and across heathland, making this a glorious free run for your dog. Take time to visit the striking village of Woodhall Spa, with its stunning 1920s architecture, boutiques and Jubilee Park.

Lincolnshire – A Dog Walker's Guide

Terrain

Easy, flat trails.

Where to park

There is a car park at Ostler's Plantation. **OS map:** Explorer 273 Lincolnshire Wolds South (GR: TF 216 629/Sat Nav: LN10 6YU).

How to get there

From The Broadway, the main road through Woodhall Spa, turn down Kirkby Lane opposite the golf club. After two miles is a Caravan Club site on your left. Immediately afterwards on your right is an unmarked entrance into the woods car park.

Nearest refreshments

There are three pubs nearby, all with beer gardens for Muttley. The Blue Bell Inn, Tattershall Thorpe, LN4 4PE is an old thatched cottage pub, steeped in Dambusters' history and popular for food. The Mall, Station Road, Woodhall Spa, LN10 6QL is on the main broadway. Ebrington Arms, Kirkby-on-Bain, LN10 6YT is a 16th-century inn and again, popular for food service.

The Walk

● ●

1 From the noticeboard in the car park, go straight ahead for 100m before turning left at the first picnic bench. Follow this long stretch of track past heathland until you reach the fence at the end.

2 Turn right and walk alongside the fence line by **Kirkby Moor Nature Reserve**. Follow this path as it curves to the right and continues past heathland.

Dog factors

Distance: 2½ miles.
Road walking: None.
Livestock: None.
Stiles: None.
Nearest Vets: Ian P. Laird, Sandy Bank Road, Coningsby LN4 4YE ☎ 01526 342265

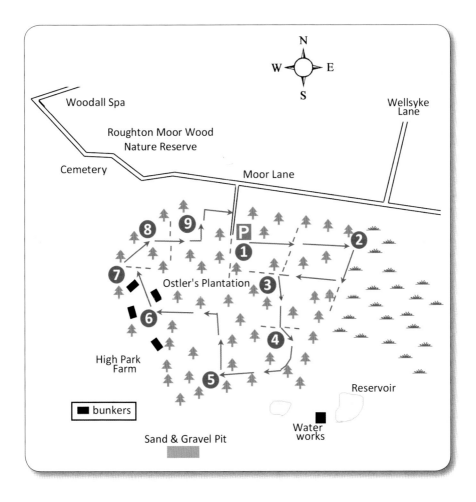

3 At the first main crossroads, turn left and follow the path past towering pine trees. After a while the path bends round, but stay ahead until you meet the Y-junction shortly afterwards.

4 At the Y-junction, turn left and walk towards the edge of the wood. Just before you reach the end of this path, pick up the trodden path that bears right into the wood and begins to follow the fence line. There are lovely views across the countryside from this part of the walk. Continue to follow this trail, keeping your eyes open for the **disused brick bunker** on your right from the days when this was a Second World War airfield.

5 After 50m from the bunker, the path through the wood reaches another path crossing it. Now turn right and follow the new path, past another bunker. Continue as the path becomes concrete and curves to the left towards another bunker. Keep to the path round the back of the bunker to a T-junction at the end.

6 Turn right and follow the path round, passing a brick wall and continue to follow this path through the woods.

7 Follow the main path through the edge of the woods, passing another bunker, set back from the path on your left. Follow this path until you meet a large tree with a faded path circling it.

Enjoying the view!

8 Turn right, following the path deeper into the woods. After 200m, you meet a crossroads in a clearing and walk straight ahead, back into the woods. This path now opens up into a large grassy track.

9 At the next crossroads, turn left, and after 50m, the path forks. Bear right on to the woodland path which weaves through trees before going back on to the main path. Bear right, crossing the path as it splits, then left into the wood, following the path. Continue all the way back through the wood to the car park.

Ancient woodland at Stapleford Wood

Running out of the woods.

This is a lovely walk which offers a beautiful guided tour of Stapleford Wood, Stapleford Moor and Stapleford village. It combines a peaceful woodland walk with a ramble across arable farmland, with plenty of variety and streams for your dog to splash and play in. This area is hidden amongst some of Lincolnshire's prettiest villages. It would be a good idea to bring an OS map with you for this walk as there are many trails through the woods.

Lincolnshire – A Dog Walker's Guide

Terrain
Can be muddy underfoot in some areas after wet weather.

Where to park
There's a Forestry Commission car park in the middle of Stapleford Wood.
OS map: Explorer 271 Newark-on-Trent (GR: SK 858 561).

How to get there
Newark is the nearest town. From the A17, follow signs towards Stapleford village. The wood is very large and has several parking areas. The main car park is well signposted on your left.

Nearest refreshments
There is sometimes a concession stand serving refreshments in the car park. For an excellent beer garden, there's The Green Man at Norton Disney, LN6 9JU (dogs are only allowed outside). Otherwise, the 300-year-old coaching inn, The Dovecote at Swinderby, LN6 9HN allows dogs in the bar and has a pleasant dog walk behind the pub. Both are highly rated for their service and food.

The Walk
. . . .

1 You will see a path either side of the information board in the car park. Take the path on your right and continue ahead through a pathway of trees marked by white marker posts. When you get to the first crossroads of a graded track, continue ahead. This section of path can be very muddy underfoot after wet weather.

Dog factors
. . . .

Distance: 5 miles.
Road walking: small amount on a country road.
Livestock: None.
Stiles: None.
Nearest Vets: Newman Watters, The Old Turk's Head,
231 London Road, Balderton, Newark NG24 3HB
☎ 01636 701523

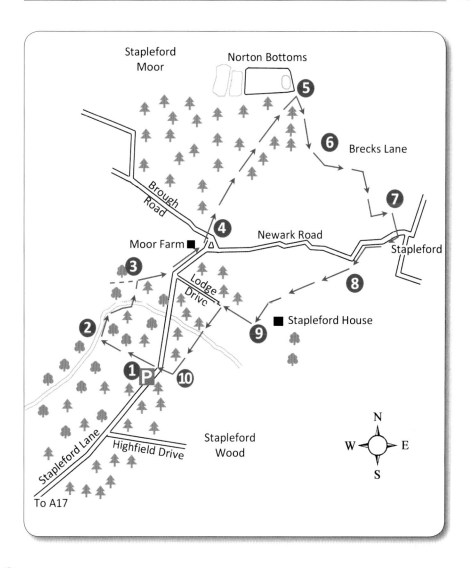

2 At the next crossroads by the boundary of the woods, turn right. There is a stream at this crossroads which your dog might enjoy. Continue ahead with the stream on your left. As you walk along, you will notice an area of new tree planting on your right and at the end of this section, you rejoin the graded track turning left which crosses a small bridge over the stream – another good spot for dogs!

3 Follow the path as it curves to the right. As you approach the end of the road, you will see a gate with a way-marker and a hamlet of houses. Continue through the gate and on to the road. Continue ahead, then left on to the country road. Follow the road around for approximately 300m until you reach a triangular junction with a Give Way sign. Turn left at this junction, heading towards **Stapleford Moor**.

4 After 10m turn right into the woods, picking up the footpath again. As you head into the woods, you will notice a **No Public Access** sign on your right. You continue to follow the footpath through the woods then follow the footpath round. When you reach a T-junction, continue ahead. After a while, the footpath opens up, with a field on your right to walk along the edge of Stapleford Moor.

5 Head out into a clearing and continue ahead. At the crossroads, continue ahead by the way-marker sign. At the end of this pathway is a diagonal crossroads. Walk ahead through the woodland by the way-marker. There are a few way-markers along this stretch to follow and at the end of this path there is a Public Bridleway sign. Turn right as you walk along this section, which can be muddy underfoot. There is a small river on your left – another water spot for dogs!

6 When you reach a crossroads, continue ahead. At the next T-junction, stay forward. At the end of this path is a beamed gate where you walk around it, passing an arable field. We now head out of **Stapleford Moor** along a section of arable farmland known as **Brecks Lane**. At the end of this bridleway you meet a tarmac road that curves round to the left along a row of cottages in **Stapleford village**.

7 Follow the road around this small village until you reach a T-junction then turn right onto **Newark Road**. You pass **Poplar Tree Farm** on your left as you walk along. This is a section of country road, so be vigilant when approaching a 90° bend to the right by the crash barrier. You will see a public footpath sign leading off on the left to follow.

8 Continue along the public footpath known as **Moor Lane**, which runs between two arable farming fields. Follow this long path until you see Stapleford House on your left beside a public footpath signpost. Also on your left is a rifle range.

9 Turn right at the public footpath sign back towards **Stapleford Wood**. You are now heading down **Lodge Drive**, a tarmac road into the woods, and you might hear the occasional distant gunfire from the rifle range. Take the second path on your left, a main forestry track, which passes a wooden locked gate and follow this path. After a few metres you will cross a clear stream, which is an excellent place for the dogs to cool off. At the end of this path there's a wooden beam swing gate.

10 Cross the gate and at the T-junction, turn right. Advance 100m to another swing gate which leads onto the main road, **Stapleford/Coddington Lane**. Cross the road, and this leads you back to your starting point.

Enjoying a swim.

Freiston Shore

Heading inland.

Freiston lies in the Wash region of the county, an atmospheric area of marshlands and wetlands. This part of the landscape is what makes Lincolnshire so varied, and offers a great opportunity to observe an abundance of bird life on the wetlands. This walk at Freiston Shore takes you around the lagoon rift, with the incessant noise of birds on the water. It explores this curious landscape and its sea banks before heading back inland through trees and arable farms. Your dog will enjoy having the wind in his face as he runs across the embankments!

Terrain

The flat wetlands area can be muddy underfoot in some areas.

Where to park

Freiston Nature Reserve has its own free car park beside the Plummers Place Guesthouse. It is sign posted. **OS map:** Explorer 261 Boston (GR: TF 398 424/ Sat Nav: PE22 0LY).

How to get there

From the A52 east of Boston, is the Castle Inn at the junction of Haltoft End. Turn here on to Church Road for Freiston and continue to follow this road past the village and Coupledyke Hall. Bear right towards signs for Freiston Nature Reserve and pass Scrane End. Once you see the Plummers Place Guesthouse on your right, you will see the sign for the car park.

Nearest refreshments

The Ball House, Wainfleet Road, Fishtoft, PE21 9RL on the A52 (just after Johnson's garden centre) is a very dog friendly pub. Dogs are allowed inside this cosy pub and in the lovely rear beer garden. Check the website as it does have restricted opening hours: www.theballhouseboston.co.uk

There are two other pubs nearby where dogs are allowed in the beer garden: The Kings Head, Freiston, PE22 0NT is a cosy 17th-century pub with outside seating. The Bull & Dog, Freiston, PE22 0LA is recommended for its food.

The Walk

. . . .

1 You start this walk by the Nature Reserve noticeboard in the car park. When facing the noticeboard, turn right. You will see a sign for a **Lagoon Trail** and follow this path, which passes a bird hide with dog parking facilities outside.

Dog factors
. . . .

Distance: 4½ miles.
Road walking: Only on a quiet track.
Livestock: There might be cattle at point 2 and a field of friendly horses at point 3.
Stiles: 3.
Nearest vets: Marshlands Veterinary Centre, Field Street, Boston PE21 6TR ☎ 01205 363073 (East side of Boston)

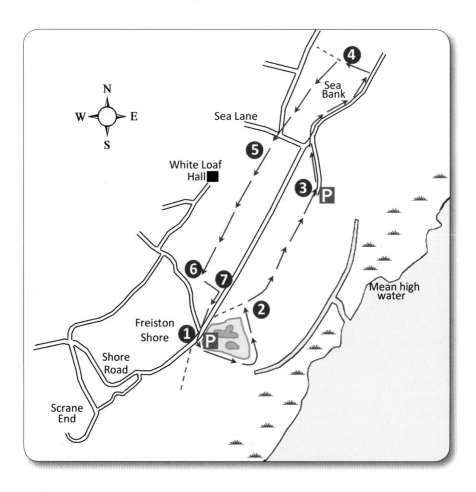

Continue past a view point. Next you reach a set of steps leading up to the embankment and from here bear left to an area that can be muddy underfoot after wet weather. Continue ahead and after 50m you meet a wooden fence with a left-pointing arrow. Turn left and pass the information board.

2 The lagoon is on your left-hand side as you walk along the embankment with excellent views of the wetlands and bird life. Continue along the embankment until you reach a wooden fence and gate. Bear right along this area known as **The Delph**. This section of embankment can have a small amount of grazing cattle in it, so keep your dog on a lead if you pass any. At the end of this embankment is a wooden gate and stile to cross into a car park.

3 From the car park continue towards the road and follow it round. (There is a footpath on the higher embankment if you prefer to use it, but it is very over-grown). This quiet road leads you round to a public footpath sign where there is a gated road for farm access and a field of horses. Cross the stile into the field where there are friendly horses, with your dog now on a lead. At the other end, cross the stile on to the track.

The lagoon at Freiston Nature Reserve.

4 Turn left at the footpath sign which leads you across a track onto a narrow grassy path through the trees. At the end of this path is a public footpath sign by a T-junction where you turn left.

5 This path leads you through an enclosure of trees. At the end of this path is a road beside a cottage. Bear right towards the footpath sign and turn left. This takes you through a grassy embankment. Continue to follow this path, which leads you down and up a set of wooden steps. You will notice **White Loaf Hall Farm** approaching on your right and you cross a farm track down a second set of wooden steps, before continuing back up some steps to the embankment.

6 Bear left with the path as it curves round. You will see a set of large market garden greenhouses on your right called **West View**.

7 At the end of the embankment, you meet a quiet access road. Turn right. You will pass the **Coastguard Cottages** here on your right. Further ahead are cottages on your left, beside the public footpath sign. Leave the road, following the footpath back to the lagoon and the car park.

The Vale of Belvoir

Peaceful moment at Muston Lock.

For anyone who hasn't yet discovered this stunning area on the Lincolnshire border, you are in for a treat! This walk is best done in spring or summer, when the fields are at their most golden, the tracks are not muddy, and the wildlife is at its most abundant.

This walk guarantees you and your hound a beautiful day out in the countryside. Your dog will love the opportunity to swim in Grantham Canal as you enjoy the peaceful stroll along the towpath. I strongly recommend you make the most of your day by stopping for lunch at the Rutland Arms at the half-way point. Here you can sit beside the canal on a sunny day and enjoy the views. Your dog will appreciate this dog-friendly pub. Afterwards, a ramble beside arable farmland and through the wooded Shipman's Plantation will lead you back to the village. It's worth stopping at the Old Forge Tearooms, where you can enjoy some refreshments in their garden beside the stream.

Terrain

Can be muddy underfoot in some sections after rainfall.

Where to park

Park on the roadside by the market cross monument. **OS map:** Explorer 247 Grantham (GR: SK 827 376).

How to get there

From the A52, between Bottesford and Sedgebrook, turn off at Muston. Drive through the village, bearing left. At the junction opposite the church, turn right. At the next junction, turn left. Park along this section by the old stone cross.

Nearest refreshments

The Dirty Duck at Woolsthorpe-by-Belvoir NG32 1NY sits at the halfway mark of this walk. It has outdoor seating beside the canal, hot and cold food served daily and is dog friendly. It also has a children's play area. The Old Forge Tearooms on Main Street in Muston NG13 0FB is perfect on your return. It offers indoor and outdoor seating, is dog friendly and is in a tranquil setting. The Gap Inn, Muston. NG13 0FD. This pub with its popular carvery sits on the A52.

The Walk

. . . .

1 From the market cross, walk towards the edge of the village in a south-westerly direction. You will approach a junction called **Woolsthorpe Lane**. Here there is a signpost with a horseshoe on it, marking it as a byway. Follow this path, it can be muddy underfoot after wet weather. Continue for about 300m until you approach a sign on your left welcoming you to **Muston Meadows National Nature Reserve**. *There is a notice advising dog owners to keep dogs on a lead whilst crossing the reserve to 'keep the skylarks singing'.* Cross the style into the nature reserve and walk diagonally across the first field *'muckheap'* towards a gate. Go through the gate into the second field *'Longore'*, again walking diagonally across the field towards the gate at the other end by a way-marker and reserve sign.

2 Go through the gate where you will see **Longore Bridge**. From here you meet the **Grantham Canal**. Turn left and begin to follow the towpath. You will find benches along the way for rest-stops. This section is a lovely spot for your dog to enjoy a splash and a swim and in spring and summer, you can spot swans and their cygnets.

Dog factors

Distance: 5¼ miles.
Road Walking: 600m on a quiet road.
Livestock: None, covers only arable farmland.
Stiles: Three.
Nearest Vets: Avenue Veterinary Centre, 1 Queen Street,
Bottesford NG13 0AH ☎ 01949 843277

After half a mile, you approach **Muston Bridge**. Continue along the path which takes you under the bridge into a beautiful part of the canal walk. You now pass the weir at **Muston Lock**.

The canal path continues all the way to the halfway point. The next lock is Stenwith Bottom (13), then Stenwith Top Lock (14), Stenwith Bridge (15), Woolsthorpe Lock (16) and from lock 16 you approach the **Dirty Duck** on the opposite side of the canal.

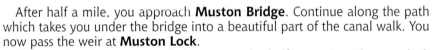 Turn right to cross the bridge towards the **Dirty Duck**. Here you can enjoy a rest beside the canal. When you are ready to continue, cross the bridge and head towards a second bridge almost immediately. Go under the second bridge and continue ahead, where your path sits between two arable fields. There is a sign urging dog owners to keep their dogs off the farmland.

Continue along this track as it curves into an S-bend and at the end you meet a T-junction. The footpath signs have been removed, but the posts still remain for **Longmoor Lane**. Turn left and remain on this track until you meet the road. As you approach **Woolsthorpe Lane**, a quiet country road, put your dog on the lead for this next section.

4 Turn left at the road and walk 600m until you near a single-lane bridge up ahead. To your right is a track beside a field marked Field View Paddock. Turn up the track, following this for ¾ mile, walking beside **Shipman's Plantation**, part of The Viking Way national path. Sometimes you can spot foxes in this area.

5 When you leave the woodland, you will see a row of cottages on your left. Turn left after the cottage following the public footpath sign. Follow the road as it bends to the right and continue ahead. You pass **Sedgebrook Mill** on your left with its large solar panels. Continue ahead, with the fields remaining on your right.

6 Towards the end of the field, you will see a small woodland with a way-marker sign on your left. Turn left into the woodland, and cross a small path towards a stile. Cross the stile into the meadow and follow the left-side path down towards the village. (The other path leads to the church). After walking

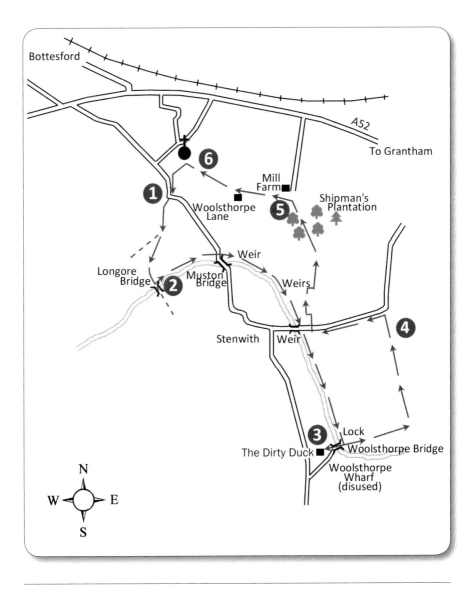

down the hilly meadow, you meet a marker post by a narrow wooden bridge. Cross the bridge over a stream, another good place for your dog to cool off and have a drink. Continue ahead through the small lane back towards the village. At the end you will see the stone cross from the start of your walk.

Now is the time to have a well earned rest at the Old Forge Tearooms!

Lincolnshire's stunning summer farmland.

The Hills & Hollows
by Grantham

Meadows filled with wild poppies.

This walk is dog heaven and once you've done it, you'll be coming back time and time again. It shows how you can find some of the most beautiful walks just on your doorstep while being only a short stroll from the town centre. This hilltop paradise overlooks Grantham in its peaceful ambience, while St Wulfram's church proudly dominates the skyline. For your dog, there is the freedom to stroll safely the whole way round and explore the woodlands known locally as 'The 'ills & 'Ollows', run across the meadows and meet other like-minded dogs. The Parish Council have put benches in place to make this a lovely picnic spot and it also makes a stunning sunset walk.

Lincolnshire – A Dog Walker's Guide

Terrain

Good all-weather walk. Flat and even terrain as you start at the top of the hill.

Where to park

Verge-side parking near the top of Cold Harbour Lane/Spring Hill **OS map:** Explorer 247 Grantham (GR: SK 928 352/Sat Nav: NG31 7TW)

How to get there

The Hills & Hollows is a hidden gem. It is on the eastern side of Grantham. From the A52 (coming from the east), drive past the Prince William of Gloucester Army Barracks and down Somerby Hill. At the bottom of the lane on your right is a Shell garage and immediately after is Cold Harbour Lane. Turn up here and follow the road to the top. Alternatively, coming from the A52 from the west, drive all the way through Grantham, passing McDonald's on your right and continue towards the Shell garage on Somerby Hill on your left. Just before the garage is the 'no through road' sign, where you turn left and follow the road to the top.

Nearest refreshments

The Fox and Hounds, Old Somerby. NG33 4AB allows dogs in the beer garden.

Syston Fruit Farm, Nr Grantham, NG32 2BZ (on the A607 heading east) has outdoor seating at the café. Belton Garden Centre, opposite Belton House on the A607 just outside Grantham, allows dogs in the outdoor seating area in the new and extended restaurant.

The Walk

• •

1 From the end of the track where you are parked, turn left through the green

Dog factors

Distance: 2½ miles.
Road walking: None.
Livestock: None.
Stiles: None.
Nearest vets: Avenue Veterinary Centre, 35 Avenue Road, Grantham NG31 6TJ ☎ 01476 563371

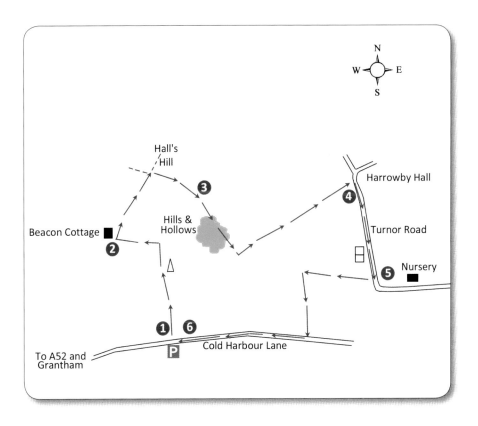

metal gate marked 'private property' (no vehicles allowed) and walk along the track. The hedge-line will be on your right and you will walk past three fields on your left, which are fenced off.

2 The track curves to the right and comes to an end as you pass the second fenced off field and approach **Beacon Cottage**. Here there is a public footpath sign and a wooden gate. Turn right, passing the cottage and follow the track as it becomes a grassy footpath, known as **Lady's Walk**. Continue along the field edge until the footpath begins to fork. Bear left, heading down and up through a small covering of trees. Continue ahead, enjoying the views of the town on your left, especially the 13th-century St Wulfram's church. Towards the end of this field, the footpath begins to fork again. Turn right, where you will notice a large fallen tree on your left and the fenced off Hills & Hollows in the distance. Continue along this path until you reach the end of this section of field.

The hill at the top of the town.

3 The Hills & Hollows is clearly marked with its Parish Council notice and has a picnic table. There is a public footpath sign just before you enter it through the wooden gate and stay ahead on the footpath, bearing left all the way through. At the end is another wooden gate as you leave this area.

Leaving the Hills & Hollows, bear left immediately where after 20m you meet another wooden gate. Go through the gate and begin to walk along arable farmland. There are excellent views of Belton House and Londonthorpe Wood from here. Continue along this path as it steadily becomes a track and leads you to the end of the field by a closed metal gate between two houses. Walk around the gate and on to the road. This is **Harrowby Hall Estate**.

4 There is a restricted byway sign and you turn right on to **Turnor Road** (unadopted) and walk along this quiet access road alongside arable farmland.

5 Towards the end of this road, it begins to bend to the left beside two houses. and there is a public footpath sign. Turn right, following the narrow footpath through the hedgerow. Towards the end of this path, it forks. Bear left and continue to follow the footpath around the edge of the field until the footpath begins to curve to the right. After 20m, there is a large opening in the hedgerow on your left. Go through this and turn right to walk along the edge of the arable field with the hedge line on your right. There are excellent views of the south-west side of town from here.

6 At the end of this side of the field is a metal gate and an opening in the hedgerow ahead. Go through the opening which leads you to turn right back on to the track. Turn left, and you will see the verge-side parking.

Ingoldsby, Boothby and Kirton Woods

View over Kirton Wood.

This walk takes you through a beautiful part of the Lincolnshire Vales, walking through woods and strolling by golden cornfields. The countryside views are stunning and you stroll by some of the vale's prettiest villages. There are plenty of places to enjoy a picnic en route and your dogs will love the freedom of the wide open countryside and exploring deep into Ingoldsby Wood.

Terrain

This flat ground can be muddy underfoot in some places.

Where to park

From Ropsley, with The Green Man pub on your left, turn right after 20m down Crown Hill. Follow the road all the way down until you meet a triangular junction on the edge of farmland. Verge-side parking here. **OS map:** Explorer 247, Grantham (GR: SK 993 328)

How to get there

Take the A52 east out of Grantham and turn off following the signs to Ropsley.

Nearest refreshments

The Green Man in Ropsley, NG33 4BE is a pub and tea room. It has a good reputation for food and won 'CAMRA Pub of the Year' in 2017. Dogs are allowed in the beer garden. The Fox & Hounds, Old Somerby. NG33 4AB allows dogs outside in the beer garden.

The Walk

. . . .

1 From the triangular junction, turn left and follow the track with Kirton Wood on your right in the distance. When you reach the crossroads there is a public footpath and a 'No motor vehicles allowed' sign. Continue ahead as the track turns into a grassy bank. The path skirts through a small wood which can be very muddy underfoot after wet weather. Continue ahead as you enter an enclosed path between field boundaries. You then pass a public footpath sign on your left and again, walk ahead. The path opens up into a field by a way-

Dog factors
. . . .

Distance: 5½ miles.
Road walking: None except to cross one quiet country road.
Livestock: None, though you may come across horses being ridden on the public bridleway.
Stiles: 3.
Nearest Vets: Kirks Vets, Old Grantham Barracks, Sandon Road, Grantham NG31 9AS ☎ 01476 574304

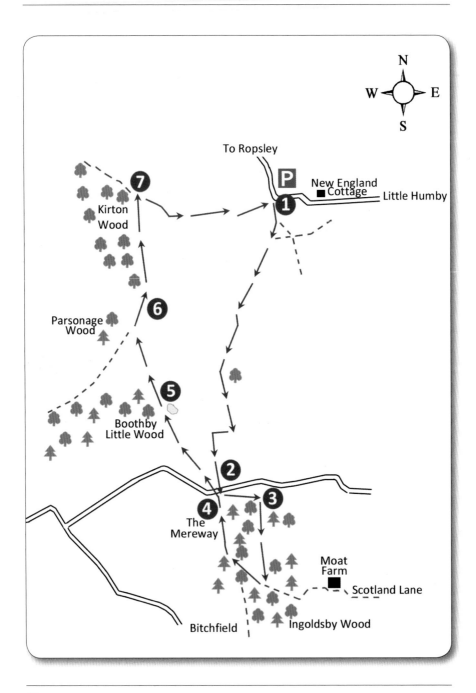

marker sign. Turn right. At the end of this section of path, you meet a road where you turn right.

2 Cross the road, and then turn left towards the public bridleway sign. Continue down the track for about 100m until you see a metal gate on your right. Opposite the gate is small path leading into the woods beside a wooden gate. Take this path which weaves easily by the edge of **Ingoldsby Wood**. It can be muddy underfoot in parts of this wood.

On the edge of Ingoldsby Wood.

3 Take the first path that branches off to a grassy clearing on your right near a pond. This section can be excellent for deer spotting. Follow this wide path all the way to the bottom until it meets the road. Now turn left and follow the track down, passing a turning area on your right. Take the next right path with a yellow marker and follow it through a trail which leads up to a wooden fence and stile. The path bears right just before the stile, so stay on it, following this woodland trail until it merges on to the track by a way-marker. Turn right. Follow the grassy track along to a wooden barrier by a public bridleway sign and continue ahead down the track as you leave **Ingoldsby Wood**.

4 At the end of the track you meet a road. Cross the road and continue ahead on to a grassy path by a public footpath sign. As the field opens up, you follow the footpath across a field towards **Boothby Little Wood**. At the end of the field is a way marker and a name (**Danelaw Way**). Join the graded track on a bend and continue ahead. You now skirt the edge of **Boothby Little Wood** and remain on the track.

5 As you pass the end of the wood, there is a small pond on your right which your dog might enjoy. Continue ahead with the hedge on your right towards **Parsonage Wood**.

6 As you reach the edge of the field by Kirton Wood, turn right to cross a wooden footbridge, then left into the field and walk diagonally across the footpath. At the end of the field, cross the wooden footbridge and turn left, following the track on the edge of **Kirton Wood**.

7 At the end of Kirton Wood is a public footpath sign. Turn right into arable farmland and right again, following the field edge as it bends to the left. The hedge line should be on your right. At the end of this field, cross the stile by the public footpath sign. This takes you to a graded track. Turn right and you are back at your start point.

A river walk by Surfleet Seas End

Enjoying the riverbank.

This walk offers a chance to view the delightful Fens village of Surfleet. The river Glen runs alongside your walk, giving you a wonderful view of the dozens of pontoons and boats docked at the end of gardens. And your dog has the opportunity for a dip in the water. The route passes arable land and flower-filled meadows with plenty of space for an energetic hound. There are three riverside, dog-friendly pubs along your route making this 'there and back' walk (although not quite 'circular') perfect for a lunchtime stroll.

Good all weather walk. Flat, even terrain.

Where to park

Roadside parking by St Lawrence's church opposite the Mermaid Inn. Notice the medieval church spire which leans by 6ft, due to soft fenland soil. **OS map:** Explorer 249 Spalding & Holbeach (GR: TF 251 282/Sat Nav: PE11 4AB)

How to get there

Travelling south along the A16, 4 miles from Spalding, turn right before the bridge into Surfleet, where there is a brown tourism sign 'Riverside'. Drive all the way through the village until you reach St Lawrence's church at the T-junction.

Nearest refreshments

Spoilt for choice! The Mermaid Inn is the first riverside pub, followed by The Riverside and at the halfway point is The Ship, and they all have outdoor riverside seating. The Ship is very dog-friendly and allows dogs inside, too.

The Walk

- -

1 From the Mermaid Inn, use the pavement which crosses the bridge, then turn left and cross the road. You will see a sign **The Brown Fen Waterway Trail**. Walk between a house and a riverbank until you reach a large garden. Walk along the riverside edge of the garden which leads you to an arable field. The field widens into a track and from here you can admire the views of the river, and all the boats tied up on their pontoons at the end of gardens. You come to

Dog factors

- -

Distance: 4¾ miles.
Road Walking: Short sections to cross roads.
Livestock: None.
Stiles: None.
Nearest Vets: The Alder Veterinary Practice, 58 Bourne Road, Spalding PE11 1JW ☎ 01775 766646

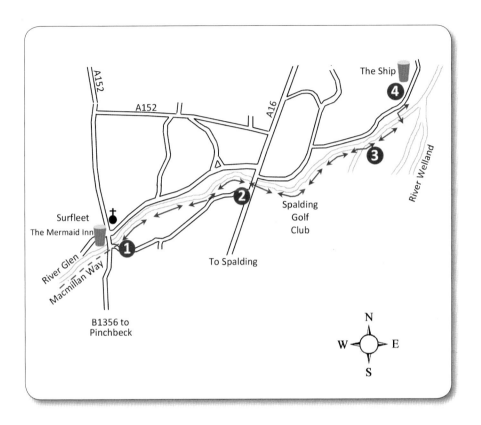

Surfleet Slipway when you see two picnic benches and an information board about the area. Continue ahead, following the Macmillan Way markers.

2 As you view **The Riverside pub** on your left, you reach a bridge for the A16. Use the underpass, putting your dog on a lead, before bearing left on the other side. This leads you through the golf course. There is a sign for dogs to be on a lead when crossing the golf course. Stay to the far left of the golf course and walk past the bungalow, before rejoining the riverbank. Continue along this far left side for almost 1 mile until you reach a large shed at the end.

3 At the end of the golf course, go through a metal gate and cross a bridge over **Blue Gowt Drain** into a field. Turn left along a concrete road before you walk around a swing gate. Turn left down to a grassy path which leads between the chalets and the riverside.

4 As you reach the bridge (sluice), climb the steps up to the road, turn left and cross the road at the end of the bridge by a footpath sign, following the embankment. You have reached the halfway point when you see the benches on the embankment outside **The Ship**. A perfect place to stop for lunch. Return by the same route.

The river Glen at Surfleet Seas End.

Ponds and adventure at Bourne Wood

Playing by the water.

This ancient woodland is a mix of conifers and broadleaf trees, which together with well laid paths, makes this an excellent spot for all-year-round dog walking. This walk is a good introduction to Bourne Wood and dips between the quiet woodland tracks and surfaced paths. The first part of this walk explores the hidden winding tracks around this lovely area. A real treat for an adventurous dog! It has a halfway point marked by two ponds, surrounded by picnic benches for a rest-stop and a swim for your dog.

Terrain

Good all weather, all year walk. Generally a flat, even terrain with some slight climbs. Can be muddy underfoot in some parts of the wood off the main path.

Lincolnshire – A Dog Walker's Guide

Where to park
Free Forestry Commission car park at Bourne Wood. **OS map:** Explorer 248 Bourne & Heckington (GR: TF 075 201).

How to get there
The wood is well signposted on the A151, 1 mile west of Bourne.

Nearest refreshments
The Black Horse Inn at Edenham, Grimsthorpe PE10 0LY is a beautiful 17th-century coaching inn. The Five Bells at Edenham PE10 0LL is a 19th-century inn with a classy modern interior but not open all day. Both country pubs are on the A151 with large beer gardens.

The Walk

● ●

1 From the car park, walk into the woods through the two wooden sculpture arches and turn left. Continue to the junction by the noticeboard. There are several paths leading off this area. Take the second path on your left by a public footpath sign, leading uphill after the main track. This path through the woods takes a steady climb for around 400m. Cross over the first crossroads junction and continue until you near the edge of the woods. Around 10 m before you reach the bend to the right, there is a path on your right with a **red/blue marked post**. Turn off here and follow the trail which rejoins the top path further up from the bend, effectively cutting the corner. This is a good area for blackberry picking and you bypass Pillar Wood on your left (Private Wood).

2 Continue along the woodland path until you meet a crossroads by an **orange marked post**. Turn left and follow the short trail through the depths of the

Dog factors

● ●

Distance: 3 miles.
Road Walking: None.
Livestock: None.
Stiles: None.
Nearest Vets: Exeter Veterinary Centre, 15 Exeter Street, Bourne PE10 9NW ☎ 01778 422863

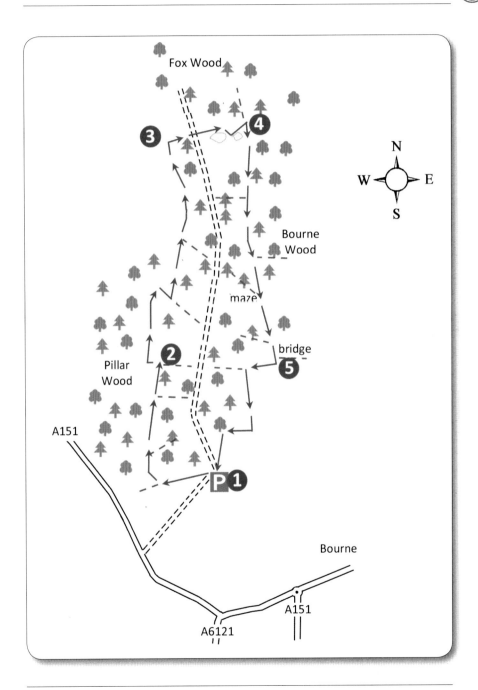

wood, exploring this quiet little-used area. If you're lucky you may see deer in these parts of the wood. This path takes you to the edge of **Pillar Wood**.

Strolling through Bourne Wood.

3 At the end of this path is a T-junction, Turn right and walk downhill towards another T-Junction. Again, turn right leading to a bench by another crossroads. Turn left here. Follow the path as it crosses a way-marked crossroads. Continue ahead. The path then begins to climb and bends to the left. Pass the first junction on your right. Follow the top path as it tracks alongside arable farmland and through the trees on your left, until you reach the top of the track by a crossroads. Turn right, and follow the large grassy track downhill to the bottom where you should meet a bench on the main track. At the bench, cross the track and continue ahead along a grassy bank for about 150m until you see an opening in the trees and a path leading off from the right. You are now at **The Ponds**, the halfway point. It makes a very pleasant stop here where your dog can have a swim and a drink. Feel free to explore this area before you leave.

4 When you are ready, follow the path beside the two benches on your left (from where you came in). Bear left and then right until you reach the T-junction which takes you back on to the main track. By the signpost for **Beech Avenue**, turn right and follow this long section of path all the way down until you come to an **orange marked post** by a public footpath sign.

5 Turn right here, going back into the woods. Take the next left by the **orange marked post**, and the next right by another **orange marked post** beside a small wooden bridge. Continue to follow this path as it weaves through the wood, bearing right at the end by the next **orange marked post**. This trail now leads back towards the main path beside the noticeboard. Take the second path (straight ahead) and follow this past a **blue post** and back towards the wooden sculpture arches by the car park.

Riverside walking by the Welland

Meadows beside Uffington Park.

This is a beautiful riverside walk nestled between two picturesque stone villages on the south Lincolnshire border. The beginning of the walk takes you through woodland and by the edge of the river, before crossing the bridge to continue down the other side through delightful meadows looking out to majestic Burghley House. Your dog will welcome the many opportunities to dive into the river Welland, while you can enjoy the peace and stunning landscape of this tranquil stroll.

Terrain

Good all weather walk on flat, even terrain.

Where to park

Verge-side parking and spaces on the right of the bridge. **OS map:** Explorer 234 Rutland Water (GR: TF 066 068).

How to get there

This walk begins between the villages of Uffington and Barnack on the south-east outskirts of Stamford. From the A1, leave at the A43 by Stamford (following directions to Burghley House). Follow this road through Stamford until you reach a T-junction, turn left, then immediately right towards 'Barnack and Burghley House'. Follow the road to Barnack, turning left in the village on to Uffington Road (towards Uffington). Over a railway crossing and shortly afterwards you approach a single-lane bridge over the river Welland. Do not cross the bridge. There is parking on the verge side and to the right of the bridge.

Nearest refreshments

Ye Olde Berte Arms, Uffington, PE9 4SZ is a lovely thatched 17th-century cottage pub with a beer garden. It's open all day and serves food. Well behaved dogs are allowed in the bar at the landlady's discretion.

The Millstone Inn at Barnack, PE9 3ET is a beautiful stone village pub with a beer garden and serves food, though it is not open all day. Dogs are allowed in the bar at the landlord's discretion.

The Walk
· ·

1 Walk in a southerly direction away from the bridge (the other side has right

Dog factors
· ·

Distance: 3¼ miles.
Road Walking: Only at the beginning to cross towards the start point.
Livestock: Sheep in one field in the middle of the walk.
Stiles: 2 (one with dog gate).
Nearest Vets: Burghley Veterinary Centre, St Leonard's Street, Stamford PE9 2HU ☎ 01780 762109

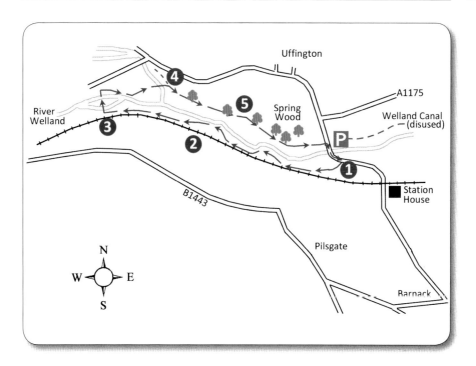

of way for cars) and walk approx 15m until you come to a public footpath sign on your right. There is a gate with a sign to keep dogs on leads around livestock if there is any in the field. Go through the gate and walk across the field to the next gate. Go through the second gate where you walk into a meadow with two pylons. Follow the path of the power lines until you reach the second pylon, then turn left, heading towards the railway track. As you reach the railway track, turn right (the track will now be on your left). Where the meadow comes to an end, turn right towards a marked gate up a small embankment. (This area can get overgrown, covering the sign.) At the top of the embankment you reach the **Torpel Way**. Turn left and begin to follow the footpath through the trees. You will see the river Welland through the trees on your right.

2 After about 200m you meet an opening on your right, with a **'Woodland Welcome'** sign inviting walkers to use the path alongside the river. Turn right here, enjoying the new path alongside the river. It makes a semi-circular detour, bringing you back into the woodlands on to the **Torpel Way**. Turning right back on to the **Torpel Way**, continue ahead until your see a second sign **'Woodland Welcome'**. Turn right, again following the semi-circular

route along the river beside new tree planting. This is a beautiful section, where swans and dragonflies can be seen. At the end of it, it leads back into the woodland. Turn right, back onto the **Torpel Way**. Shortly after rejoining, the path begins to occasionally stray beside the railway track with only a ditch between the embankment and the track. You know your own dog, so be aware if he's the type to wander towards it. On the other side is a fenced-off field with livestock. At the end of this footpath is a fence and a bench. Turn right and go through the metal gate, heading towards the concrete footbridge which crosses the river Welland. This is the halfway point and makes a lovely picnic stop.

Time for a dip!

3 Follow the footpath after the bridge which heads straight to a wooden bridge with a metal gate. Cross the bridge, turning right down a footpath. After about 100m, you meet a metal gate. Go through a wooden gate on the left of it, which enters a field where you may sometimes find sheep grazing. Walk across the field, staying ahead on the trodden path (through the middle) as you are no longer following the river.

4 At the end of this field, cross a stile to a wooden footbridge which crosses the narrow river Gwash. This is good place for your dog to drink and take a dip. Go to the stile at the end of the bridge (this one has a dog gate), which leads into a meadow on the **Uffington Park estate**. Walk ahead through the meadow towards the bridge at the end and with the fence line on your right. When you reach the wooden bridge, do not cross it. Instead turn right through a gate and follow the footpath.

5 You are now walking alongside the disused **Welland Canal**, now just a ditch. You will see views of Burghley House in the distance as you follow this footpath all the way back to the start of your walk. At the end, you reach a gate which leads you back on to **Uffington Road** beside the bridge.